CAREER EXPLORATION

Cosmetologist

by Tracey Boraas

Consultant:
Vi Nelson
Director
Cosmetology Advancement Foundation

CAPSTONE BOOKS
an imprint of Capstone Press
Mankato, Minnesota

Capstone Books are published by Capstone Press
151 Good Counsel Drive, P.O. Box 669, Mankato, Minnesota 56002
http://www.capstone-press.com

Library of Congress Cataloging-in-Publication Data
Boraas, Tracey.
 ˙ Cosmetologist/by Tracey Boraas.
   p. cm.—(Career exploration)
   Includes bibliographical references and index.
   Summary: Introduces the career of cosmetologist, providing information about
educational requirements, duties, the workplace, salary, employment outlook, and
possible future positions.
   ISBN 0-7368-0592-3
   1. Beauty culture—Vocational guidance—Juvenile literature. [1. Beauty
culture—Vocational guidance. 2. Vocational guidance.] I. Title. II. Series.
TT958 .B67 2001
646.7'2'023—dc21   00-022447

Editorial Credits

Leah K. Pockrandt, editor; Steve Christensen, cover designer; Kia Bielke, production
   designer and illustrator; Heidi Schoof and Kim Danger, photo researchers

Photo Credits

Cosmetology Advancement Foundation, 23
Frances M. Roberts, 11 (bottom), 33
Index Stock Imagery, cover; Index Stock Imagery/Todd Powell, 36
International Stock/Wayne Sproul, 19
Pivot Point International, 20, 26, 29, 30, 39, 41
Unicorn Stock Photos/Jeff Greenberg, 6, 42; Ron Jaffe, 9; Tom McCarthy, 11 (top),
   15; D&I MacDonald, 12; Florent Flipper, 16

2 3 4 5 6 06 05 04 03 02

Table of Contents

Career Title	Cosmetologist
O*NET Number	68005A
DOT Cluster (Dictionary of Occupational Titles)	Service occupations
DOT Number	332.271-010
GOE Number (Guide for Occupational Exploration)	09.02.01
NOC Number (National Occupational Classification-Canada)	627/648
Salary Range (U.S. Bureau of Labor Statistics, Human Resources Development Canada, and other industry sources, late 1990s figures)	U.S.: $11,510-$45,822 **Canada: $6,900-$44,000** **(Canadian dollars)**
Minimum Educational Requirements	U.S.: varies Canada: varies
Certification/Licensing Requirements	U.S.: required Canada: required

Subject Knowledge

Customer and personal service

Personal Abilities/Skills

Understand written and diagram instructions for applying hair coloring and permanent waving solutions; adapt a procedure to an individual customer's physical features; use a variety of tools such as scissors, tweezers, combs, curlers, and blow dryers; add and subtract to mix solutions in proper proportions; see differences in shapes, widths, and lengths of lines when cutting hair and shaping eyebrows; deal pleasantly with all kinds of people; use hands and fingers skillfully to wrap hair around rollers, and comb or brush hairstyles

Job Outlook

U.S.: faster than average growth
Canada: fair

Personal Interests

Accommodating: interest in catering to the wishes of others, usually on a one-on-one basis

Similar Types of Jobs

Beauty consultant; wig specialist; beauty supply distributor

Chapter 1

Cosmetologist

Cosmetologists provide personal care services. Some cosmetologists also are called hairstylists or beauticians. Cosmetologists help people improve their appearances. Many cosmetologists provide hair care. Some cosmetologists also provide nail, skin, or other services.

Cosmetologists' Duties

Most cosmetologists offer a variety of hair care services. They cut and style their clients' hair. Clients are people who use a cosmetologist's services. Many cosmetologists color their clients' hair. They apply solutions to hair to change the color. Cosmetologists also straighten curly hair and give permanent waves to straight hair. Cosmetologists often advise clients how to care for their own hair.

Many cosmetologists color their clients' hair.

Some cosmetologists specialize in certain services. Manicurists file, shape, and polish clients' fingernails and toenails. Estheticians provide skin care. Electrologists remove unwanted facial or body hair. Shampooers wash and condition hair. Makeup artists specialize in applying makeup.

Cosmetologists perform various tasks. They maintain records of the services they provide to their clients. They include notes about their clients' likes and dislikes. Cosmetologists want to build a clientele of satisfied customers. To do this, cosmetologists must remember each client's personal preferences. Cosmetologists also clean up their own work stations. They sometimes sell hair products and other supplies. They also may schedule appointments for themselves or the salon.

Tools

Cosmetologists use a variety of tools. They use some of these tools to work with hair. Cosmetologists use a plastic or cloth drape to cover clients' clothes. They seat clients in a chair that can be raised and lowered. Cosmetologists raise or lower clients so they can work more easily on their hair. Cosmetologists use combs,

Makeup artists apply makeup on clients.

picks, and brushes to comb through hair. They use scissors, razors, and hair clippers to trim and cut hair. They use rollers, curling irons, and blow dryers to style hair.

Cosmetologists also use many kinds of hair styling solutions and chemicals. They use products such as shampoo, conditioner, and styling gel. They use bleaches and tints to color hair. They apply chemical solutions to curl, wave, or straighten hair.

Cosmetologists have a specific tool or product for every procedure they perform. They use nail clippers and files to give manicures and pedicures. They apply nail polish to fingernails or toenails during these procedures. They also use nail polish remover to remove any old polish. They work with makeup tools such as brushes and sponges. Some cosmetologists use electrically charged needles to remove unwanted facial and body hair.

Working Conditions and Schedules

Cosmetologists usually work in pleasant surroundings. They usually work in clean and well-lighted salons or department stores. Some cosmetologists provide services in settings where people cannot travel to a salon. These cosmetologists may work in residential care centers, hotels, or on cruise ships.

Cosmetologists' work schedules can vary. Many cosmetologists work full-time. But some work part-time. Cosmetologists often work evening and weekend shifts. Salons often are busiest at these times.

About 40 percent of all cosmetologists are self-employed. These cosmetologists have their own salons, work in their own homes, or go to clients' homes.

Esthetician

Estheticians specialize in cleansing and improving the appearance of the skin. They give facials, full-body treatments, head and neck massages, and offer hair removal with wax treatments.

Electrologist

Electrologists use electrolysis machines to remove unwanted hair.

Manicurist

Manicurists give manicures and pedicures. They file, shape, and polish nails. They often add artificial nails.

Shampooer

Shampooers wash and condition hair. They usually work in large salons.

Chapter 2

Day-to-Day Activities

Cosmetologists have varied schedules depending on where they work. Daily work routines also vary depending on cosmetologists' specialties.

Cosmetologists at Salons

Some cosmetologists work for salons. Salon employees are assigned hours and days to work. They also are assigned clients to serve. Cosmetologists usually provide their own scissors, combs, clippers, blow dryers, and curling irons. The salon provides shampoos and other products.

Cosmetologists employed by salons are responsible for many duties. They may maintain

Some cosmetologists work for salons.

the salon and supplies. They may prepare the cash register at the beginning of each day. They make sure the cash register has a specified amount of money in it.

Cosmetologists prepare cleaning solutions for the salon tools. Every comb, scissors, and brush must be sanitized after each use. Sanitizing kills germs that can spread disease or skin disorders. Cosmetologists also fold towels and drapes.

Cosmetologists' duties vary from day to day. For example, a cosmetologist may give nine haircuts, a facial, and two permanent waves one day. The next day, the cosmetologist may give three manicures and 14 haircuts. Cosmetologists often serve between 10 and 20 clients each day. They clean up their work stations after each procedure. They sweep up hair on the floor.

Salon cosmetologists also have other duties. Some cosmetologists may sell hair or skin care products to clients. Cosmetologists also may operate the cash register. They accept payment from clients for services. Cosmetologists also may answer phones and schedule appointments.

Cosmetologists' duties may vary from giving manicures to styling hair.

Some cosmetologists help close salons. They clean and disinfect tools such as combs, scissors, and curling irons. They empty wastebaskets. They restock supplies. They may close out the cash register. They remove all the cash, count it, and record the amount.

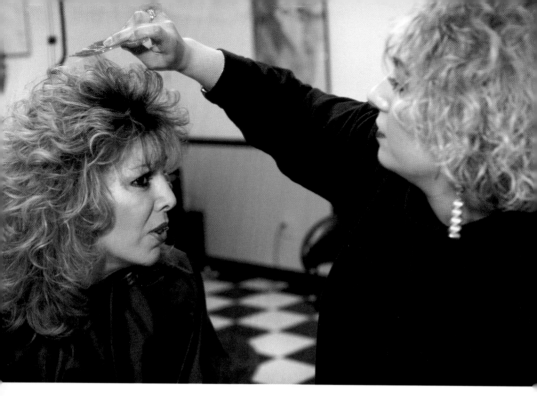

Independent cosmetologists often supply their own tools and supplies.

Independent Cosmetologists

Self-employed cosmetologists are independent cosmetologists. Most independent cosmetologists rent a chair and work area at a salon. Independent cosmetologists set their own appointments and work schedules. They sometimes establish their own rates for services. Some independent cosmetologists provide a variety of services.

Others specialize in services such as skin treatment. Cosmetologists who are independent cosmetologists establish their own clientele.

Independent cosmetologists usually supply their own tools and supplies. Some independent cosmetologists also furnish their own hair and skin care products. They also provide their own cleaning solutions to clean their tools. Some salon owners provide cleaning and hair care products. But independent cosmetologists usually must pay salon owners for the products that they use.

Independent cosmetologists perform many of the same tasks as cosmetologists who are salon employees. But they also have some additional duties. They order their own supplies and products. They also keep track of the product inventory. This list includes all of the products the salon has in stock.

Independent cosmetologists maintain their own accounts and do their own bookkeeping. Independent cosmetologists need a manager's license. They also need their own malpractice insurance. Malpractice insurance provides money to be paid to clients if procedures are not performed properly.

Salon Owners

Many cosmetologists own their own businesses. Some have small salons in their homes. Others operate large salons. Salon owners may work alone, hire employees, or use the services of independent cosmetologists. Salon owners must have malpractice insurance. They are legally responsible for the services provided at their salons by themselves and their employees. Salon owners are not responsible for the services of independent cosmetologists.

Cosmetologists who own small salons usually perform cosmetology services throughout the day. Their daily activities are similar to those of independent cosmetologists or employees. They schedule their own appointments and maintain their own supplies and records. They clean their work areas. Many also sell hair, nail, and skin care

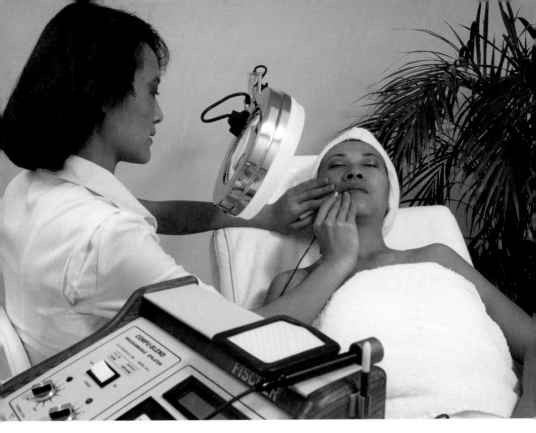

Salon owners hire cosmetologists.

products. Salon owners must maintain records as well as supply and product inventories.

Cosmetologists who own large salons need a manager's license. Salon owners hire other cosmetologists. They supervise and train several cosmetologists.

Chapter 3

The Right Candidate

Cosmetologists need both technical and social skills. They must know how to perform various services for their clients. They also must work well with other people.

Interests

Cosmetologists should enjoy helping people. They talk with their clients about what services they want. Cosmetologists must follow their clients' wishes.

Cosmetologists should enjoy working with hair and beauty products. They should enjoy using these products and their skills to improve their clients' appearances.

Cosmetologists should be interested in style and trends. Trends are new or popular ideas or

Cosmetologists must work well with people.

styles in hair and beauty. Cosmetologists need to know how to create popular hairstyles. They also may need to be familiar with nail and makeup trends.

Abilities

Cosmetologists must enjoy learning new skills. They must update their skills by attending classes and seminars each year. They need to be familiar with the latest styles and trends. They also may need to learn how to provide the latest hair and skin procedures.

Cosmetologists must use good judgment when performing procedures. Chemicals applied to hair incorrectly can damage hair. Poor haircuts can take months to grow out. Cosmetologists and their employers can be held responsible if a service turns out poorly. The salon or its insurance company may have to pay the client for the damage or perform the service again.

Cosmetologists must be able to give advice to clients. They need to suggest styles that would be most attractive on each client. They should know clients' individual needs.

Cosmetologists need to be aware of clients' needs.

Cosmetologists must have good form perception. They need to accurately see the lengths of hair as they cut or style it.

Cosmetologists also must be good at recognizing color differences. They should be able to select makeup and hair colors that look best on clients.

Cosmetologists should be able to deal pleasantly with all types of people. Clients may have difficulty making decisions about services

Skills

Workplace Skills   Yes / No

Resources:
Assign use of time .... ☑ ☐
Assign use of money .... ☑ ☐
Assign use of material and facility resources ...... ☑ ☐
Assign use of human resources .... ☑ ☐

Interpersonal Skills:
Take part as a member of a team .... ☑ ☐
Teach others .... ☑ ☐
Serve clients/customers .... ☑ ☐
Show leadership .... ☑ ☐
Work with others to arrive at a decision .... ☑ ☐
Work with a variety of people .... ☑ ☐

Information:
Acquire and judge information .... ☑ ☐
Understand and follow legal requirements .... ☑ ☐
Organize and maintain information .... ☑ ☐
Understand and communicate information .... ☑ ☐
Use computers to process information .... ☑ ☐

Systems:
Identify, understand, and work with systems .... ☑ ☐
Understand environmental, social, political, economic,
    or business systems .... ☑ ☐
Oversee and correct system performance .... ☐ ☑
Improve and create systems .... ☐ ☑

Technology:
Select technology .... ☑ ☐
Apply technology to task .... ☑ ☐
Maintain and troubleshoot technology .... ☐ ☑

Foundation Skills

Basic Skills:
Read .... ☑ ☐
Write .... ☑ ☐
Do arithmetic and math .... ☑ ☐
Speak and listen .... ☑ ☐

Thinking Skills:
Learn .... ☑ ☐
Reason .... ☑ ☐
Think creatively .... ☑ ☐
Make decisions .... ☑ ☐
Solve problems .... ☑ ☐

Personal Qualities:
Take individual responsibility .... ☑ ☐
Have self-esteem and self-management .... ☑ ☐
Be sociable .... ☑ ☐
Be fair, honest, and sincere .... ☑ ☐

they want. This can be frustrating. Cosmetologists must deal with clients in a pleasant manner.

Technical Skills

Cosmetologists need to be very careful and exact in every procedure they perform. For example, some cosmetologists are skilled at performing electrolysis. They must be careful in order to remove the hair without harming the client. Cosmetologists also must be careful when they apply color solutions or permanent waves to hair.

Cosmetologists know how to perform a variety of services. They style hair in different ways. Some cosmetologists provide hair and scalp treatments. Some give facials. Some cosmetologists offer manicure services. They also may apply makeup. Cosmetologists need to skillfully perform the services they provide.

Cosmetologists need business skills. They often sell products in salons. Business skills also are important for cosmetologists who want to operate their own salons. These cosmetologists often must keep inventory, accounting, and tax records. Cosmetologists who employ other cosmetologists also need management skills.

Chapter 4

Preparing for the Career

People who want to be cosmetologists need to prepare for the career. They need to receive training to perform cosmetologist duties. Most cosmetologists also need to be licensed in the state or province where they work.

High School Education

Most people who want to be cosmetologists should have a high school diploma. Most state licensing boards require a high school diploma. But other states only require cosmetologists to be at least 16 or to have completed the eighth grade.

In Canada, people usually can enter the Hairstylist Apprenticeship Program after they

Cosmetologists must receive proper training for their career.

have completed the 10th grade. Each province has its own apprenticeship program. Students in apprenticeship programs take high school classes to earn credit toward graduation. They also work part-time in salons as apprentices. Apprentices work under the direction of licensed cosmetologists. After graduation, they may work full-time as apprentices until they complete the program.

Students who want to be cosmetologists should take a variety of high school courses. Students learn about the properties of chemical solutions in chemistry classes. Art classes help students understand color and design. Students learn a variety of math skills in math and business courses. English and speech courses teach students to communicate effectively.

Post-Secondary Education

Training programs for cosmetologists vary. Some programs last eight months. Others may last more than two years. Many vocational schools offer cosmetology programs. States or provinces license vocational schools. In

Many vocational and other post-secondary schools offer cosmetology training.

Canada, some employers are willing to accept trained cosmetologists as apprentices. In some provinces, people may complete post-secondary education programs instead of hairstyling apprenticeship programs. But employers still may require on-the-job training.

Post-secondary cosmetology programs often include classroom study, demonstrations, and practical experience. Courses include anatomy

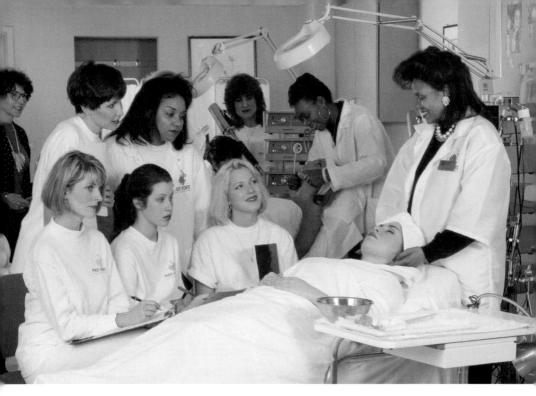

Training includes demonstrations in different cosmetology techniques.

and physiology. These classes teach students the structure of the human body and how it works. Students also learn about hygiene, sanitation, and different skin conditions. Students learn how to use and care for cosmetology tools. Cosmetology students also take business courses. These classes teach students how to keep business records, manage employees, and sell products.

Cosmetology training includes cosmetology technique demonstrations. Students learn how to perform different services by watching instructors perform these duties. Most schools teach students how to work with male and female clients. Male and female clients often have different skin and hair care needs.

Cosmetology students practice the various procedures. They first practice on mannequins. They then practice on clients. These clients pay a small fee for cosmetology services at school salons. Instructors closely supervise students throughout the procedures.

Apprenticeship Program

In Canada, people who want to become hairstylists may need to complete an apprenticeship program. Apprenticeship requirements in each province vary. Apprentices in most provinces need a 10th-grade education. People entering apprenticeship programs also must find employers willing to hire and train apprentices. Apprentices learn their skills by working for certified and experienced workers called journeypersons. These people have completed an apprenticeship or training program. Cosmetology apprentices also take classes at a vocational or trade school.

Cosmetology apprenticeships usually last two to three years. Apprentices earn money while they train. They may earn between 50 and 65 percent of the journeyperson pay rate. Apprentices must take an exam after they complete their apprenticeship program. Apprentices receive a provincial journeyperson certificate after they pass the exam. This document enables them to work as hairstylists in the province.

In the United States, students can complete an apprenticeship program instead of attending a post-secondary school. But few cosmetologists complete an apprenticeship program. The U.S. Department of Labor Bureau of Apprenticeship Training (BAT) offers an apprenticeship program for cosmetologists. The BAT is the federal agency responsible for registering various apprenticeship programs.

Cosmetologists' licensing and certification requirements vary by state or province.

Licensing

In the United States, training program graduates must take a state licensing test. The test includes written and practical sections. During the practical section, applicants perform cosmetology procedures. Licensing officials judge applicants' cosmetology skills.

In Canada, certification and licensing requirements vary by province. Hairstylists may

High School Diploma

Apprenticeship
(Mainly Canada)

be required to complete an apprenticeship program and obtain trade certification. Trade certification qualifies people to work as journeypersons in their career field. Hairstylists must take a provincial exam to receive the certification. This exam includes written and practical sections.

Some provinces require provincial licenses for skin care specialists and manicurists. Other provinces do not require licenses for these specialists.

In Canada, some cosmetology students or apprentices take the Interprovincial Standards Exam (IPSE) after they complete their training program. Those who pass the exam receive the Red Seal. This license allows them to work in other provinces.

Cosmetology Training	Licensing

Continuing Education

Cosmetology careers require years of continuing education. Hairstyle trends change often. Manufacturers invent new hair and skin products. Cosmetologists must know the latest styles and techniques.

Cosmetologists have many opportunities to continue their education. They may attend training sessions offered by cosmetology schools or salons. Cosmetology equipment and product manufacturers offer training on the use of their products. These companies often host product shows. Cosmetologists can learn about manufacturers' products at these events. Cosmetologists also may attend workshops offered by cosmetology associations.

Chapter 5

The Market

The job market for cosmetologists is expected to remain favorable. Population growth and a strong economy will create more job opportunities for cosmetologists. Cosmetologists will be needed to advise clients about different styles, products, and services.

Salary

Average earnings for full-time cosmetologists and hairstylists vary. They may be paid an hourly rate or a salary. Some cosmetologists work on commission. Their pay is based on how many clients they serve. Commissions often depend on the prices salons charge for services. Cosmetologists receive part of the price charged for each service. Some cosmetologists who

Cosmetologists will be needed to advise clients about different styles, products, and services.

work on commission also receive a small salary. Cosmetologists' salaries also may depend on the supplies and tools provided by the employer. Employers who provide many service supplies may keep a larger share of the money earned.

Cosmetologists often receive tips from clients. Cosmetologists usually are allowed to keep these extra amounts of money. But tips are considered income. Cosmetologists must pay taxes on any tips they receive.

Cosmetologists in the United States usually earn between $11,510 and $45,822 per year. The average salary is between $25,480 and $38,563 per year.

Most cosmetologists in Canada earn between $6,900 and $44,000 per year. The average salary is between $19,100 and $24,800 per year.

Salon cosmetologists usually receive a wage. They often receive tips from clients. They sometimes also receive commissions. As employees, salon cosmetologists may receive benefits such as insurance and sick leave.

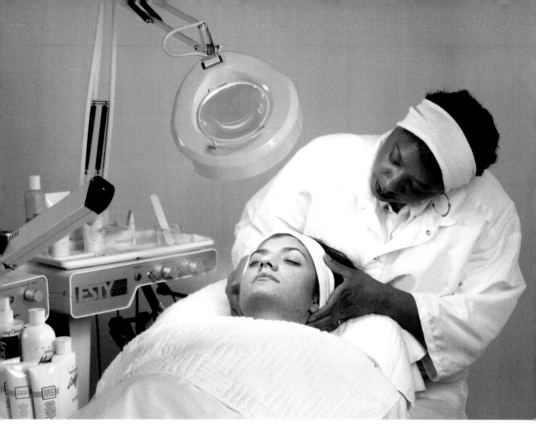

Cosmetologists have many employment opportunities.

Job Outlook

Employment opportunities for cosmetologists are expected to grow. In the United States, job opportunities are expected to have above-average growth. In Canada, the job market is expected to remain fair. The demand for cosmetology services will continue to increase with the growth and aging of the population. A strong economy also contributes to more job opportunities. People will have more money to spend on themselves as incomes continue to increase.

Cosmetologists licensed to provide a wide range of services will find many job opportunities. But competition for jobs is greater at salons that are well known or offer higher salaries. Opportunities for part-time and self-employed cosmetologists will continue to grow. The demand for skin care and nail services also will remain strong.

Advancement and Related Careers

Cosmetologists may advance as they gain experience and continue their education. Cosmetologists usually earn more money as they build a larger clientele. Some cosmetologists advance to management positions. They may manage large salons with several employees. Other cosmetologists may open their own salons.

Some cosmetologists become instructors at cosmetology schools.

Cosmetologists also have other advancement opportunities. Some cosmetologists move into teaching positions at cosmetology schools. Others become wig specialists. These people make wigs for companies or clients.

Some experienced cosmetologists work as examiners for state licensing boards. These

people make decisions about the qualifications of new cosmetologists.

Cosmetologists or people interested in the field have other career opportunities. Some become sales representatives for hair care or cosmetic companies. These people also may work for beauty supply distributors. They sell products to cosmetologists, salons, or stores. Others work at makeup counters at department stores. These people focus on selling products rather than applying makeup.

Cosmetologists or other individuals may open businesses as image consultants. These beauty or fashion consultants advise clients on fashion and beauty.

Job opportunities for cosmetologists are expected to increase in the future. Cosmetologists will be needed as hair, makeup, and other style trends change. Cosmetologists' skills will be needed to help people look and feel their best.

Cosmetologists' job opportunities are expected to increase.

Words to Know

client (KLYE-uhnt)—a person who uses the services of a cosmetologist

electrologist (i-lek-TROL-uh-jist)—a person skilled at using an electrically charged needle to remove unwanted facial and body hair

esthetician (ess-thi-TISH-uhn)—a person who provides skin care

facial (FAY-shul)—a treatment with massage to enhance the health or appearance of the face

manicurist (MAN-uh-kyur-ist)—a person who cleans, shapes, and polishes fingernails and toenails or applies artificial fingernails

salon (SUH-lahn)—a place of business where people can receive cosmetology services

To Learn More

Cosgrove, Holli, ed. *Career Discovery Encyclopedia.* Vol. 2. 4th ed. Chicago: Ferguson Publishing, 2000.

Cosmetology. Careers in Focus. Chicago, Ill.: Ferguson Publishing, 1998.

Gearhart, Susan Wood. *Opportunities in Beauty Culture Careers.* VGM Opportunities. Lincolnwood, Ill.: VGM Career Horizons, 1996.

Lytle, Elizabeth Stewart. *Careers in Cosmetology. Careers.* New York: Rosen Publishing Group, 1999.

Strazzabosco, Jeanne M. *Choosing a Career in Cosmetology.* World of Work Series. New York: Rosen Publishing Group, 1997.

Useful Addresses

Allied Beauty Association
3625 Dufferin Street
Suite 235
Downsview, ON M3K 1Z2
Canada

**American Association of Cosmetology
   Schools**
15825 North 71st Street
Suite 100
Scottsdale, AZ 85254

National Beauty Culturists League
25 Logan's Circle NW
Washington, DC 20005

National Cosmetology Association
401 North Michigan Avenue
Suite 2200
Chicago, IL 60611-4267

Internet Sites

Career Center: Cosmetologist
http://www.collegeview.com/career/careersearch/
  job_profiles/human/cos.html

Cosmetologists Chicago
http://www.isnow.com

Cosmetology Advancement Foundation
http://www.cosmetology.org

**Job Futures–Technical Occupations in
  Personal Service**
http://www.jobfutures.ca/jobfutures/noc/
  627.html

**Occupational Outlook Handbook–Barbers,
  Cosmetologists, and Other Personal
  Appearance Workers**
http://stats.bls.gov/oco/ocos169.htm

Pivot Point International, Inc.
http://www.pivot-point.com

Index